The Power of Believing

Live the supernatural, abundant life

Dr. Winferd Holt

Copyright © 2013 by Dr. Winferd Holt

The Power of Believing
Live the supernatural, abundant life
by Dr. Winferd Holt

Printed in the United States of America

ISBN 9781626976559

All rights reserved solely by the author. The author guarantees all contents are original and do not infringe upon the legal rights of any other person or work. No part of this book may be reproduced in any form without the permission of the author. The views expressed in this book are not necessarily those of the publisher.

Unless otherwise indicated, Bible quotations are taken from The King James Version.

www.xulonpress.com

Contents

1. What People Are Saying vii
2. Dedication ix
3. Acknowledgement xi
4. Foreword xiii
5. Introduction xvii
6. What the Scripture Says About
   The Power of Believing 21
7. Correct Steps to The Power
   of Believing 29
8. Unbelief 35
9. Eliminate the Causes of Unbelief 39
10. Know Who You Are 43
11. Attitude of Gratitude 47
12. Banish Belief Bombs 49
13. The Apple of God's Eye 53
14. Picture Possessing Your Desires 57
15. Correct Way to Pray 63
16. You Are a Magnet 67
17. Affirmation 73
18. 4 Vital Daily "To Do's" 77
19. Believing Exemplified 81

20. Summary 83
21. About the Author 87

What People Are Saying . . .

Dr. Holt has done a masterful job summarizing what the Bible teaches on belief and unbelief. More importantly, Dr. Holt explains how to apply these Biblical truths in our day-to-day lives to see God's people set free from poverty, illness, bondage, and the power of sin.

Dr. Richard Mays
Author, Speaker, Physician, Knoxville, TN

Here is the book you have waited all your life to read! Have you ever desired more faith? I know I have. In *The Power of Believing*, Dr. Winferd Holt reveals a biblical pattern both to increase our faith and to gain an understanding of how to embrace God's promises daily. This remarkable book is a key to living the abundant life offered in John 10:10. Thank you, Dr. Holt, for showing us the multidimensional picture of what salvation through Jesus Christ really means!

> Joy Brown
> Author, Speaker, President of Creation Kidz, Co-founder of Diversified Ministries, Myrtle Beach, SC

As a Christian speaker and author, my ultimate goal is to inspire and challenge people to read, believe, and obey the Word of God in such a way that their daily walk with God is impacted, and their daily lives are filled with Kingdom power. Dr. Winferd Holt has written a book outlining this Kingdom power—a power available to all Christians through the simple scriptural process of *The Power of Believing* and obeying the promises of God. As you read this book, you will learn practical ways to stand on the promises of God and receive all the blessings God has in store for you as a child of the King!

> Phyllis Elliott Elvington
> Phyllis Elliott Elvington Ministries, Green Sea, SC

Dedication

First and foremost, this book is dedicated to God, my Father, who revealed His message, inspired its writing, and guided my hand. I am forever grateful for His divine wisdom, understanding, and application of His Word in my every day living.

To my dear wife, Mary Lester, who was supernaturally healed by believing that God's Word is true. When critically ill, she repeatedly spoke the name *Jesus, Jesus, Jesus* out loud and believed that God was faithful to perform His Word even when medicine stated it could not be done.

To my daughter Wynne and her family: Kemp Floyd and their children, Jamin and Mary Reagan. Wynne has labored hours to proofread and correct my manuscript.

To my son Dale and his family: Tammy and their children, Trace and Logan. A mighty work God has done in their lives through His power to heal.

Acknowledgement

I would like to thank our ForYou family, the distributors in our company, who have prayed for me and have so patiently listened to me teach Godly principles. ForYou is an international, direct-sales company that markets life-changing, natural nutritional and personal care products through individuals in a home-based environment. As president and founder of ForYou, Inc., I have the privilege of touching many lives across this great nation and abroad. I believe ForYou is more than an international business; I believe it is a ministry for today. The product formulations that God allowed me to develop have a Godly influence. Many have testified that ForYou brought them closer to the Lord. Some came to receive Jesus as their Lord and Savior through ForYou. I have met thousands of dedicated believers who have become a part of our family. I would like to say a special "Thank You" to these wonderful people.

Foreword

By Dr. Richard Mays

I believe the largest single obstacle to Christians living the abundant life that Jesus has already paid in full (John 10:10) is unbelief or doubt. When Jesus gave Himself to die on the cross, He provided the grace to live a supernatural, abundant life. Grace is that which gives us, as believers, the power and authority over our environment, our situations, our weaknesses and fears, and all evil forces. Christ apportioned that grace (Ephesians 4:7) into five major categories necessary to have abundant life. There is the grace for salvation and forgiveness of sins. There is the grace for healing and living in divine health. There is grace for being set free from anything that could hold us in captivity. There is grace to restore to us everything that Satan and the world system have stolen, and there is grace to be supernaturally blessed. All the grace we need to live a supernatural, abundant life has already been given to us. There is nothing left to give. That is why Jesus' last words on the cross were, "It is finished." There is nothing left to do. It is a completed, perfect work.

The key to access this grace is faith or belief. In the Bible, certain words are interchangeable. Thus, faith and belief have the same meaning, as does doubt and unbelief. Romans 5:2 says, "We have access by faith into this grace wherein we stand." Thus, we are completely surrounded by all the grace (power and authority) that we will ever need to live a supernatural, abundant life; but, we can only access or utilize that grace by our belief (faith).

In his book, ***The Power of Believing***, Dr. Winferd Holt has clearly and accurately outlined what the Bible says concerning the power of belief. I believe this is the single most important Biblical concept to understand if we are to live the life God desires us to have and if we are to advance God's kingdom in these last days.

Dr. Holt has done a masterful job summarizing what the Bible teaches on belief and unbelief. More importantly, Dr. Holt explains how to apply these Biblical truths in our day-to-day lives to see God's people set free from poverty, illness, bondage, and the power of sin.

We all should meditate on these Scriptures recorded in this book and say them aloud every day until they change our mind, our emotions,

Foreword

our will, and even our very DNA—until we believe as Jesus did—without doubt.

Dr. Richard Mays is a board certified family physician, practicing integrative medicine in Knoxville, Tennessee. Dr. Mays is also a student of the Bible and travels extensively teaching on subjects such as faith, divine healing, and the human triad of body, soul, and spirit. Dr. Mays has conducted several healing revivals and has seen many miracles take place. Dr. Mays is the author of *The Bible Diet* which provides scientific proof that God's dietary laws are just as pertinent today as they were 6000 years ago.

The Power of Believing

If I could tell you that if you did one thing you could never fail, would you do it? What God does and what He says can never fail. God's laws and precepts will never fail. You possess the ability to operate in God's unfailing laws and precepts. One precept, perhaps the most important of God's laws, is **The Power of Believing**.

The Power of Believing is the most powerful, magnetic force on earth. It is even more powerful than atomic energy or an atomic bomb. This power is a gift from almighty God. Now, the choice is yours to use His gift correctly. The way you choose to use His gift will determine if you get results or not.

The greatest miracle and gift from God is the new birth, being born again. When you accepted Jesus Christ as your Lord and Savior, you first had to **believe**. This new birth is your salvation and confession for eternal life. True born-again Christians hold steadfast to their belief for eternal life; and when asked if they know they will go to heaven when they die, they respond, "Yes, I know that I know that I know." Did you know that Jesus Christ did even more on Calvary's cross? As a **believer**, you became joint-heirs with Christ Jesus, thereby entitling you to ALL of God's promises as found in His Word. You can experience and live in those promises today, here on earth! You can live the abundant life now! You do not have to wait until you get to heaven to experience the abundance God has in store for His people. Simply **believe** the Word of God with childlike faith to receive healing, prosperity, and all of God's blessings. You must **believe** God's promises the very same way you **believed** to receive Jesus Christ as your Lord and Savior. For everything in your life, you must **believe** the same way. Sadly to say, Satan has done a great job deceiving God's people and blinding them of **The Power of Believing**. Most Christians are denied this power either through lack of knowledge, lack of faith, or lack of believing. It is my prayer that those scales be lifted from your eyes and that the blind will see the powerful message God has revealed in this book.

There is a correct way to **believe** and an incorrect way to **believe**. Most Christians seem to be paralyzed due to unbelief, misbelief, or disbelief. Possible misunderstanding of theological principles handed down through generations or misinterpretation of our rights and privileges as Christians has rendered the crippled state of the

Christian. Do you **believe** you should prosper and be in good health? Do you truly **believe**? If you **believe** the right way, in accordance with God's Word, you will prosper and be of good health.

Let us look closely at God's Word; let us take the Word of God literally. Meditate on the following Scriptures day and night, until these Scriptures are engraved permanently, indelibly on your heart. Read and confess these Scriptures out loud. Scriptures when quoted out loud will increase your faith, for in Romans 10:17 the Word says, "faith cometh by hearing, and hearing by the word of God." This is a bold statement: when you speak the Word of God out loud and in faith, it is as if God himself spoke the Word. For we find in John 1:1, "In the beginning was the Word, and the Word was with God, and <u>the Word was God</u>."

What the Scripture Says About The Power of Believing

*The following Scriptures,
when internalized, will change your life.*

What the Scripture Says About The Power of Believing

The following Scriptures, when internalized, will change your life. You must **believe** that these Scriptures are written for you just as strongly as you **believe** the Scriptures for salvation and eternal life. **Believing** gives you the power to act on God's Word, to stand on God's Word, to confess God's Word. **Believing** releases God's ability to perform His Word. Unbelief, misbelief, and disbelief serve to derail God's plan for your life. Unbelief, misbelief, and disbelief are radical sins (departing from the living God) and stop God's ability to perform His Word for us and through us. You must **believe** (know that you know that you know):

God's Gift

> Ecclesiastes 5:19: "Every man also to whom God hath given riches and wealth,

and hath given him power to eat thereof, and to take his portion, and to rejoice in his labour; this is the gift of God."

II Chronicles 20:20: "**Believe** in the Lord your God, so shall ye be established; **believe** His prophets, so shall ye prosper."

Isaiah 7:9: "If you will not **believe**, surely ye shall not be established."

The Sin of Unbelief

Mark 9:24: "Lord, I **believe**; help thou my unbelief."

Hebrews 3:12: "Take heed, brethren, lest there be in any of you an evil heart of unbelief, in departing from the living God."

Hebrews 3:19: "So we see that they could not enter in because of unbelief."

The Power of Believing

Romans 4:20-21: "He (Abraham) staggered not at the promise of God through unbelief; but was strong in faith, giving glory to God; And being fully persuaded (belief) that, what He had promised, He was able also to perform."

Mark 9:23: "If thou canst **believe**, all things are possible to him that **believeth**."

Matthew 8:13: "Go thy way; and as thou hast **believed**, so be it done unto thee."

Matthew 21:22: "And all things, whatsoever ye shall ask in prayer, **believing**, ye shall receive."

Mark 11:24: "Therefore I say unto you, What things soever ye desire, when ye pray, **believe** that ye receive them, and ye shall have them."

Ephesians 1:19: "And what is the exceeding greatness of His power to us-ward who **believe**, according to the working of His mighty power."

God's Promises

Psalm 34:10: "but they that seek the Lord shall not want any good thing."

Job 36:11: "If they obey and serve him, they shall spend their days in prosperity, and their years in pleasures."

Psalm 92:12: "The righteous shall flourish like the palm tree."

Psalm 35:27: "Let the Lord be magnified, which hath pleasure in the prosperity of his servant."

Isaiah 53:5: "and with his stripes we <u>are healed</u>."

Psalm 30:2: "O Lord my God, I cried unto thee, and thou hast healed me."

Luke 8:50: "**believe** only, and she shall be made whole."

Jeremiah 17:14: "Heal me, O Lord, and I shall be healed; save me, and I shall be saved: for thou art my praise."

God's Will for Our Life

I John 5:14-15: "And this is the confidence (belief . . . I know that I know that I know) that we have in him, that, if we ask any thing according to his will, he heareth us: And if we know that he hear us, whatsoever we ask, we know that we have the petitions that we desired of him."

Deuteronomy 8:18: "But thou shalt remember the Lord thy God: for it is he that giveth thee power to get wealth, that he may establish his covenant which he sware unto thy fathers, as it is this day."

Jeremiah 29:11 (NIV): "For I know the plans I have for you, declares the LORD, plans to prosper you and not to harm you, plans to give you hope and a future."

III John 2: "Beloved, I wish above all things that thou mayest prosper and be in health, even as thy soul prospereth."

Scriptures for Our Present Day

Job 27:16-17: "Though he heap up silver as the dust, and prepare raiment (clothing) as the clay; He may prepare it, but the just will put it on, and the innocent shall divide the silver."

Proverbs 13:22: "the wealth of the sinner is laid up for the just."

Ecclesiastes 2:26: "For God giveth to a man that is good in His sight wisdom, and knowledge, and joy: but to the sinner He giveth travail, to gather and to heap up, that he may give to him that is good before God."

Haggai 2:7-9: "AND I WILL SHAKE ALL NATIONS, AND THE DESIRE (WEALTH) OF ALL NATIONS SHALL COME: AND I WILL FILL THIS HOUSE (**BELIEVERS**) WITH GLORY—The silver is Mine, and the gold is Mine, saith the Lord of hosts. The glory of this latter house (God's people) shall be greater than the former."

There is no question that God desires the wealth of the world to be in the hands of Christians. You need to read these Scriptures daily and **believe** them in your heart until they become a reality in your life. Your faith must be in the Word of God and not in your physical senses of touching, seeing, tasting, smelling, or hearing. It does not matter what it feels like or looks like; pay no attention to it!!! Just **believe** the Word!!!

You must confess these Scriptures out loud. Be not guilty of accepting only the portion of Scriptures that fit your personal denomination or errant teaching. You must simply and literally accept the whole Word of God as truth. You must **believe** in your heart that the Scriptures will do exactly what they say they will do for you.

> I Thessalonians 2:13: "For this cause also thank we God without ceasing, because, when ye received the word of God which ye heard of us, ye received it not as the word of men, but as it is in truth, the word of God, which effectually worketh also in you that **believe**."

Confession must be supported by belief. Without belief, nothing will happen.

Correct Steps to The Power of Believing

Every promise in the Bible is absolutely true, and every promise is yours. While 'sense knowledge faith' is important, this is not the faith that will receive God's blessings.

Correct Steps to
The Power of Believing

Your first step is to accept the Bible as the truth and nothing but the truth. The Bible is God's Word. Every promise in the Bible is absolutely true, and every promise is yours. Accept the Bible as if God is speaking directly to you.

> II Timothy 3:16-17 says, "All scripture is given by inspiration of God, and is profitable for doctrine, for reproof, for correction, for instruction in righteousness: That the man of God may be perfect, thoroughly furnished unto all good works."

The phrase "given by inspiration of God" is one word in the Greek, meaning "God-breathed" or from the mouth of God.

Begin with unwavering FAITH. You must **believe** every word. You may say you have faith, but the question is: Is your faith 'sense knowledge faith'? Do you have faith because you can touch it, see it, taste it, smell it, or hear it, or do you have the one and only true faith that produces results? We gain 'sense knowledge faith' through the teachings of educational or religious institutions as well as the customs and cultures of our heritage and society. We train our minds to believe certain doctrines, philosophies, and principles based on fact, scientific evidence, or family belief systems. The validity of this belief system lies in the tangible elements of our touch, sight, taste, smell, and hearing—all related to the senses and verifiable.

While 'sense knowledge faith' is important and serves a useful role in our existence, this is not the faith or belief that will receive God's blessings. The belief we are talking about is belief based on the Word of God. THIS IS IT, the only faith that produces Godly results. Real faith comes from accepting and believing the Bible is the Word of God. After all, the Bible IS the actual Word of God. When you accept the authority of God's Word and believe the infallible promises in His Scriptures, then the Word of God cannot fail. His Word must be fulfilled.

You may say that you believe the Bible is the Word, but when you pray and ask God for something, do you question if God will do it? Maybe you believe He will answer your prayers. However, when the answer does not come as you hoped, do you allow your sense knowledge to take over? Because you cannot touch, see, taste, smell, or hear any results, do you allow doubt to enter? This is where unbelief shows its sinful head.

Remember, Hebrews 3:12 reveals that unbelief is a terrible sin, "departing from the living God." Satan has surely deceived the Christian just as he deceived Eve in the Garden of Eden. Satan has truly robbed the Christian of the power Jesus Christ gave through His death on the cross. Satan has blinded the Christian with a false sense of faith. Most Christians give mental assent, 'sense knowledge faith', to the validity of God's Word and agree that God performed miracles in Biblical days and can perform miracles today. Yet, most Christians fall short in exercising the true authority of God's Word which requires **believing** God's promises despite circumstances, despite confirmations, despite evidence.

Unbelief cancels faith!!! Unbelief prevents you from receiving an answer from God. We saw the effect of unbelief in the Bible when a man brought his demon-possessed son to Jesus' disciples, and they were unable to cast out the demons. However, when the man brought his son to Jesus, Jesus cast out the demons. The disciples then asked Jesus why they could not cast out the demons and Jesus replied, "because of your unbelief." They had faith; yet for some reason, they allowed 'sense knowledge' to overrule.

Therefore, when you pray, <u>you must</u> **believe** <u>what the Bible says</u>. It does not matter if circumstances get worse, if pain gets worse, or if finances get worse. You must prevail by **believing** in, standing on, and confessing the Word of God. Never be influenced by what other people say unless their words totally align with the Scripture.

Always **believe** what the Bible says, not what life looks like at the moment. Be very careful at this point! Be grounded in the Word of God lest your sense knowledge take over, and you miss receiving what you asked God for.

His promises will prevail!!! No Word that has gone forth from God can return unto Him void. Jeremiah 1:12, "I watch over my Word to perform it." He will make good His Word if you dare stand on it.

Unbelief

Unbelief usually shows up in three ways: Lack of Knowledge, Disbelief or Misbelief, and 'Sense Knowledge Faith'.

Unbelief

Unbelief usually shows up in three ways:

1. **Lack of Knowledge:** This unbelief comes from a lack of knowledge about what the Bible says. Hosea 4:6 states, "My people are destroyed for lack of knowledge."

2. **Disbelief or Misbelief:** You do not **believe** (disbelief) what the Bible says, or you **believe** it is for someone else but not you. You may **believe** this is not relevant for today. You may say that was for the early church, but does not apply today. Sadly, this is being taught in many churches throughout our great nation. Misbelief comes from wrong teaching. You must diligently work to correct misbelief. You must **believe** the Bible regardless of your circumstances.

3. **Sense Knowledge Faith:** 'Sense knowledge faith' requires you to see it before

you can **believe** it. How many times have you heard someone say I will not **believe** it until I see it? Like doubting Thomas, you must see it and touch it before you **believe** it. John 20:24-29 is the story of Thomas' unbelief or 'sense knowledge faith'. Thomas said, "Except I shall see in His hands the print of the nails, and put my finger into the print of the nails, and thrust my hand into His side, I will not **believe**." Thomas was operating in 'sense knowledge faith'; he **believed** in what he could see and touch. Jesus was not pleased with Thomas' unbelief (doubt). In John 20:29, "Jesus saith unto him, Thomas, because thou hast seen me, thou hast **believed**: blessed are they that have not seen, and yet have **believed**." God will not bless this form of belief, belief based on evidence.

True faith is to **believe** without seeing or touching anything. You simply **believe** and act on what the Bible says without any evidence at all.

Eliminate the Causes of Unbelief

There are three primary causes of unbelief: Fear, Worry, and Concern. These roots of unbelief must be eliminated in order to have your prayers answered.

Eliminate the Causes of Unbelief

There are three primary causes of unbelief:

1. **Fear:** Fear is one of the most destructive forces on earth, a paralyzing force. Fear is a spirit, a demonic spirit from the enemy, Satan. Fear grips the mind of its victim and holds them prey to its destructive force. Job 3:25 should be a vivid example of the effect of fear, "For the thing which I greatly feared is come upon me, and that which I was afraid of is come unto me." Based on the spiritual laws of attraction, be particularly careful as it relates to fear. Whenever you fear something, you will attract to you the very thing you fear the most. Unfortunately, many people are filled with fear. Fear will destroy your faith. Fear counteracts your belief. Therefore, when you feel fear rising up, know that this is unbelief in action. This unbelief will

prevent answers to your prayers for fear is contrary to God's Word. We find in II Timothy 1:7, "For God hath not given us the spirit of fear; but of power, and of love, and of a sound mind." Three hundred and sixty-five (365) times the Bible tells us not to fear. That is a command to live each day of our life without fear!

2. **Worry:** Any form of worry produces unbelief. Worry is the opposite of faith. God will not hear and answer. The Scriptures warn us over and over again not to be anxious or worry about anything. Worry indicates that you are not trusting God. If you do not trust God, you do not **believe**. Proverbs 3:5 directs us to, "Trust in the Lord with all thine heart; and lean not unto thine own understanding." Leaning on your own understanding is relying on your sense knowledge. We have already learned that 'sense knowledge faith' is not true faith; therefore, you do not **believe** God or trust God.

3. **Concern:** Concern is the lowest level of worry or fear. Concern tries to mix 'sense knowledge faith' with true faith, and the result is a lack of trust and lack of belief in God. You find yourself asking God for

Eliminate the Causes of Unbelief

something, and then you become concerned. How will it work out? You begin to try to rationalize and determine how things will work out which in turn breeds worry. Before long, you begin to fear that God is not going to answer you. You have allowed 'sense knowledge faith' quietly to overcome you. This is not true faith; therefore, no answer will follow.

These roots of unbelief must be eliminated in order to have your prayers answered.

You must **believe**. God says that when you pray **believe** that you already have (possess) what you asked for. Did you get that? You must **believe** that you already have what you asked for. Then, start confessing that you have it. True belief is confessing that you have it before you actually possess it. When you truly **believe,** you will possess what you confess. Confession plays a vital role in your **believing**. I am talking about confessing out loud (verbally). Study the Scriptures, and you will see that God always confessed <u>before</u> He did anything. Everything God created He simply spoke into existence. Since you are created in the image of God, you are to do the same thing. Confess your desires; speak your desires into existence. If you do not confess it before you possess it, you do not **believe**.

Know Who You Are

*You are the righteousness
of God in Christ Jesus.*

Know Who You Are

The **Power of Believing** is the most powerful force you have. To experience this powerful force, there are some things you must know and do.

The first thing you should know is that you are the righteousness of God in Christ Jesus. This righteousness is a gift that Jesus gives to all who accept Him. You have the very nature of God, and your body is the temple of God. In the Old Testament, the Tabernacle had a place called the Holy of Holies where God abode while here on earth. Guess what? God now abides in you. This is an awe-inspiring fact. As a **believer**, your body is the temple of God.

I **believe** most people do not know or fully understand ALL that Jesus accomplished on Calvary that day. By far, the most important thing He did was to give us salvation and eternal life. Yet, He did so much more than that. He took into His body all mankind's disease and sickness so that we could be healed . . . "with His stripes we are healed" . . . that work was finished on the cross. He became poor that we might become rich. What does rich mean in the Scripture? Study the Greek; rich means rich. Many Christians seem to have a problem when it comes to talking about money. Most of this is due to wrong teaching (misbelief). You must also understand this part of Calvary. The Bible says in I Timothy 6:10, "For the love of money is the root of all evil," not money itself. When on the Cross Jesus said, "It is finished," He decreed that the gift of salvation, the gift of healing, and the gift of prosperity became yours if you will **believe**.

As a Christian, you should be living the abundant life now.
>You must **believe.**

You should be reigning as kings or queens here on earth.
>You must **believe.**

Do you truly know who you are? When you were born again, you became a new creature. When you accepted Jesus Christ as your Lord and Savior, you became a joint-heir with Christ Jesus. You became the son or daughter of God almighty. God is now your heavenly Father. You now have the DNA of God.

Attitude of Gratitude

*Live your life daily with an
attitude of gratitude.
When you start thanking God
for everything in your life,
you will see your faith
increase greatly.*

Attitude of Gratitude

Live your life with an attitude of gratitude. Begin to feel the joy of God's presence and His overpowering love. Make the joy of the Lord a priority in your life. This simple truth is so vitally important that it bears repeating. Live your life daily with an attitude of gratitude. You are the most blessed person on earth. When you start thanking God for everything in your life, you will see your faith increase greatly. Remember, the Bible says in Nehemiah 8:10, "the joy of the Lord is your strength." Allow joy to flood your life, and practice laughing every day. The Bible says in Proverbs 17:22, "A merry heart doeth good like a medicine." It is healing to your body. As you appreciate, as you love, as you are joyful, you allow God to move in your life in a mighty way. Love and appreciate everything that you are right now. First, you must love God, then love yourself, and then love your neighbor.

Banish Belief Bombs

If you desire to walk and live in a life of believing, there are some things you must stop doing.

Banish Belief Bombs

If you desire to walk and live in a life of **believing,** there are some things you must stop doing. Never criticize or blame yourself or anyone else. This may be one of the most difficult things for you to do. Natural man or man governed by 'sense knowledge faith' is prone to find fault. The typical response, when someone is guilty of criticizing and blaming, is to say, "Well, that is just the truth!" Or, "Well, I am just giving you the facts!" Really? What they are trying to do is justify their sense knowledge belief. Study the life of Jesus. The only people He condemned were the self-righteous. Remember in John 8 the woman that was caught in the very act of adultery and was brought to the feet of Jesus by self-righteous people, the scribes and Pharisees of their day. What did Jesus do? He said, "He that is without sin among you, let him first cast a stone at her." Every one of those people turned and left. Jesus then turned to the woman and said, "Neither do I condemn thee: go, and sin no more." Criticizing and blaming yourself or others are like self-destructive bombs. They will destroy your faith, cripple your ability to **believe**, and hinder God working in your life.

The Apple of God's Eye

You are His second-born son or daughter.
You are a child of the King.
He has given you kingship
in His Kingdom here on earth.

The Apple of God's Eye

Begin seeing yourself as the apple of God's eye. As a Christian, you possess the DNA of God. Is that an awesome revelation? You are His second-born son or daughter. You are a child of the King. He has given you kingship in His Kingdom here on earth, and it is given to you now. You must know the rights and privileges you possess right now! Just think about how much God loves you. Think about the price He paid for you.

So often people say if it is God's will let this or that occur. The concept of 'if it is God's will' is another tactic or ploy Satan uses to abolish the Christian's ability to live the abundant life. First of all, if that Christian **believes** the Word of God literally and if they are grounded in the Word daily, they should never have to say 'if it is God's will' because He makes His will clear in His Word. The promises we find in God's Word are His will for our life. Jeremiah 29:11 (NIV), "For I know the plans I have for you, declares the LORD, plans to prosper you and not to harm you, plans to give you hope and a future." You must know that it is God's will for you to be prosperous and healthy. III John 2, "Beloved, I wish above all things that thou mayest prosper and be in health, even as thy soul prospereth." You must know that salvation is more than a ticket to Heaven some day. You must start asking God and thanking God for manifesting in your life what He has already done on Calvary for your spiritual prosperity, health, finances, and about six thousand other blessings that are yours. Thank Him even before you receive the blessings.

When you pray and ask God for health, money, or anything else, always thank Him in advance for that in which you are praying. Never think about the lack of good health, lack of money, or lack of anything again. Do not even allow it to cross your mind! If you do, unbelief will creep in and take over. You have asked God for health and prosperity, now exercise your faith by **believing** and standing on His promises for health and prosperity, III John 2.

Picture Possessing Your Desires

*"Delight yourself in the Lord; And He will give you the desires of your heart."
Start picturing yourself already in possession of your desires*

Picture Possessing
Your Desires

"**D**elight yourself in the Lord; And He will give you the desires of your heart," Psalm 37:4 (NASB). Start picturing or visualizing yourself already in possession of your desires. This is part of **believing**. Many Biblical characters used visualization to help build and strengthen their belief [faith]. We see a beautiful example of visualizing or visual markers in Genesis 15:5 when God told Abraham to look toward heaven and count the stars. These stars shall represent Abraham's number of descendants. Abraham's visual marker was the stars in the sky.

Do you remember Jacob and the cattle and sheep? According to Genesis 30: 37-39,

> "And Jacob took him rods of green poplar, and of the hazel and chesnut tree; and pilled white strakes in them, and made the white appear which was in the rods. And

he set the rods which he had pilled before the flocks in the gutters in the watering troughs when the flocks came to drink, that they should conceive when they came to drink. And the flocks conceived before the rods, and brought forth cattle ringstraked, speckled, and spotted."

Jacob's visual marker was the rods he pilled and placed in the watering troughs to produce ringstraked, speckled, and spotted spots on the animals when the flock drank from the trough. This was Jacob's visual to multitudes of cattle and sheep. Genesis 30:43 (NLT) tells us "Jacob became very wealthy."

God's Word is so specific and so detailed for our daily living. God told Habakkuk to write the vision, make it plain upon tablets. This written vision made plain in every detail serves as a guide or blueprint to accomplish the goals and tasks as determined. If God thought it was important to write it down, do you think it is important for you to write down what you are asking God to provide?

Write down your desires; then audibly (out loud) repeat them over and over until you possess these desires. Write your vision on paper. Create a visual marker, and **believe** that you already have it in your possession. This visual marker serves as an instrument to strengthen your faith toward the goal you are accomplishing.

Place this written vision in highly visible places everywhere, so you can keep the desires of your heart before you as often as possible throughout your day. Your visual marker should reflect desires relating to your spiritual life, your health, your wealth, your relationships, and any other desires that you may have. Do not limit God. Make your visual markers BIG.

Now, feed on the Word of God. Read it daily, meditate on it daily, and digest it daily! Repeat God's Word over and over daily until it becomes a living part of you. Speak the Word out loud. Remember, speaking the Word out loud is the same as God speaking these Words to you.

It is critically important that your faith does not waver despite the circumstances. You must stand on the Word of God, not on what it may look like. There is a transfer of wealth taking place now. It is taking place whether you **believe** it or not. For you to have it, you must **believe**.

Know that the power to heal and the power to possess anything are present in you! That power is the Holy Spirit! The Holy Spirit is Christ living within you, walking and talking daily with you, guiding and directing your actions and words, empowering you to have whatsoever you shall ask! Get to know Him extremely well! This relationship will increase your **Power of**

The Power of Believing

Believing. This is **The Power of Believing**. As you increase in your **believing**, you will begin to see yourself as a magnet for health, for blessings, and for wealth.

You must remember that if you truly **believe**, you will possess what you **believe**. **Believing** is possessing. Let me repeat; **believing** is possessing!!! See yourself as healthy and wealthy. **The Power of Believing** can change every aspect of your life. You can turn weakness or suffering into strength, power, health, joy, and unlimited abundance. Everything is possible; nothing is impossible! There are no limits. Whatever you can dream or envision can be yours when you **believe**.

Correct Way to Pray

If you are in debt, never ask God to get you out of debt.

Correct Way to Pray

If you are in debt, never ask God to get you out of debt. That is the wrong thing to do. When you say debt, Satan hears and will use that against you. Speaking of or praying about debt focuses on the debt, and the debt will get worse. You can even attract debt to you. If bills are piling up, **DO NOT** think about them, instead focus on prosperity. Create a feeling of joy, and thank God for your prosperity.

Be very careful when you pray. Make sure no wrong message comes out of your mouth. Let me share a story a school teacher shared with me. She shared that her mother became deathly ill while pregnant with her. The medical prognosis was that her mother had blood clots, which required surgery immediately. The doctors recommended removing her mother's legs and part of her intestines. Hearing this distressing news, her mother's father went out into a corn field and began praying. He prayed that God would spare his daughter and heal her. He asked God to heal his daughter until she could raise her daughter. God answered that prayer, and her mother was healed immediately. Her mother remained healed until the daughter (the school teacher) reached nineteen years of age. The very next day her mother died suddenly of the very same illness she had nineteen years earlier. The lesson is to be careful how you pray.

You Are a Magnet

Everything in the universe has a magnetic field of attraction. Your thoughts have a magnetic attraction that will attract what you think about.

You Are a Magnet

Everything in the universe has a magnetic field of attraction. I was in Israel once standing at the entrance to the Qumran Caves where the Dead Sea Scrolls were found. The magnetic force was so strong that the hair on my head stood straight up. You have a field of attraction that attracts all things to you. This field of attraction is controlled by your thoughts. You either block or attract everything to you by your thoughts.

Your thoughts have a magnetic attraction that will attract what you think about. As you send out thoughts, you will attract to you what you are thinking. As a man thinketh in his heart, so is he. In **The Power of Believing**, your thoughts direct how you **believe**.

Money also has a magnetic field of attraction. You are a magnet; therefore, you have an attraction for money. You can either attract or block money by your thoughts. Think about the money you desire; then see the money coming to you. Never think of the lack of money, not even for a single second; ALWAYS think of the abundance of money. Never think or speak of the lack of money again. If you do, you will always be in a state of lack.

Be clear and specific about the amount of money you desire to receive. Visualize yourself receiving, giving, and using all the money you desire as if you already have it. Never think about the amount of money you can earn; ALWAYS think about the amount you would like to receive. Remember in Deuteronomy 8:18, it is God who gives you power to get wealth. Matthew 6:33 tells us to "seek ye first the kingdom of God, and his righteousness; and all (no exclusions) these things (health, wealth, and spiritual gifts) shall be added unto you."

Some say money is the root of all evil, but the Bible says in I Timothy 6:10, "For the love of money is the root of all evil; which while some coveted after, they have erred from the faith, and pierced themselves through with many sorrows." Here, we clearly see that it is the love of money, not money itself, that causes one to err from their faith resulting in much sorrow. Money or the possession of money as such is not evil. They even used the system of commodity money in Biblical times. Throughout the Old Testament, God blessed His people, Abraham, David, and King Solomon, with great wealth. Even when great Biblical men like Joseph and

Job experienced much hardship and suffering, God restored them even greater than they were before. Read the account of Joseph in Genesis 37:24-41:41 and of Job in Job 42:9-16.

Do not love money! For it is the love of money that leads one into covetousness, jealousy, and greed. Throughout time, the love of money has caused man to lie, cheat, steal, embezzle, and even murder. The love of money creates an idolatry relationship thus elevating money as a god. Anything (including your family, your spouse, your career) that is first in your life other than God, breaks God's first commandment: "Thou shalt have no other gods before me," Exodus 20:3. Satan uses this love of money to create the ultimate deception and resulting sin: man wandering away from his faith and belief in God, becoming self-sufficient, and falsely relying on his own might and strength.

Now that we have drawn a distinction between God's original intent for prosperity and Satan's subtle distortion in creating evil through the love of money, let us look at God's goodness as intended. Everything we have is a gift from God as shown in

> James 1:17: "Every good gift and every perfect gift is from above."

> Ecclesiastes 5:19: "Every man also to whom God hath given riches and wealth,

and hath given him power to eat thereof, and to take his portion, and to rejoice in his labour; this is the gift of God."

III John 2: "Beloved, I wish above all things that thou mayest prosper and be in health, even as thy soul prospereth."

Be grateful for the money you already have. Thank God for everything in your life including health, wealth, and all of God's blessings. All of God's blessings are God's gifts to His children, your inheritance from your Father. The supernatural, abundant life was intended to be lived here on earth as well as eternally.

John 10:10: "I have come that they may have life, and that they may have it more abundantly."

1 Corinthians 2:9: "But as it is written, Eye hath not seen, nor ear heard, neither have entered into the heart of man, the things which God hath prepared for them that love him."

Ephesians 3:20: "Now unto him that is able to do exceedingly abundantly above all that we ask or think."

Do you desire that your children live in financial lack or be unhealthy throughout their life? Why would you think it is God's will for you to live this way? This way of thinking in not Biblical. If we desire more for our children, then how much more does our Heavenly Father desire for His children?

There is no limit to the power of God, and as His child, it is your right and inheritance to live that abundant life. Allow not your faith to waver. **Believe** in God's truth, His Word, and His promises. **Believe** and possess your inheritance. God delights in the prosperity of His people, which includes prosperity spiritually, physically, and financially.

The key is seeking God diligently, serving Him faithfully, and **believing** that He will perform His Word. Above all things, give God all the honor, all the glory, and all the praise for what He has done, for what He is doing, and for what He is going to do for you.

Affirmation

*Affirmation is the confession
of your belief
before the confirmation
of your possession.
Affirmation is speaking it
before the fact.*

Affirmation

Affirmation is the confession of your belief before the confirmation of your possession. Affirmation is speaking it before the fact. When you speak it before the fact, you truly **believe** it. On the other hand, confirmation is speaking after the fact. NO faith or belief is required to confirm something.

Think, speak, and act as if you are already wealthy. Affirm to yourself daily that God has given you the power to obtain wealth. Affirm daily that you have money in abundance, and that money comes to you in abundance. Affirm that money comes to you effortlessly. **Believe** that money is yours and that you deserve it. Continue affirming this out loud. Thank God for a 100-fold return NOW!

Believe that you are living in the time for the transfer of wealth from the wicked to the righteous. **Believe** that you are the righteousness of God in Christ Jesus and that you deserve to receive this transfer of wealth. You must **believe** that you will receive this transfer. If you do not, the person next to you who does **believe** will receive the transfer and not you.

You must KNOW that you are worthy of this abundance because you are a child of the King. You are the righteousness of God in Christ Jesus. That, in and of itself, is enough to be excited. Continually praise God for the outpouring of His abundance on your life. Get emotional about it. Be excited for this abundance of health and prosperity. Do whatever it takes to feel excited. Remember to repeat out loud, over and over, that you are a magnet for health, a magnet for money, and a magnet for abundance. **You must do this process even before anything is manifested.**

4 Vital Daily "To Do's"

Believing is a powerful power.
Gratitude is so important.
Give thanks for what you desire.
Visualize what you desire.

4 Vital Daily "To Do's"

Believing is a Powerful Power: You must **believe** you already possess the health, the wealth, and the blessings.

Gratitude is So Important: Always thank God for what you already have, and you will attract more to you. Thank God verbally, orally. When you speak it out loud, Heaven then moves to bring it to pass. This is a very important aspect of **believing**.

Give Thanks for What You Desire: Thank God even before you receive what you desire. This will cause God to move mightily in your behalf.

Visualize What You Desire: Create a clearly defined, vivid picture in your mind of what you desire, and visualize yourself already enjoying having it. Continue this visualization until you possess what you desire. Write down in sentence form exactly what you desire, and begin each sentence with "I am so grateful that I have _____."

Always remember that **believing** is thinking, speaking out loud, and acting as if you already have it. **Believing** thoughts attract what you are thinking about. Always remember that good health comes to you the very same way you attract money. Realize that when Jesus said, "It is finished" on the cross that day, He meant it was finished. There is nothing more for God to do. It has already been done; it IS already done. It is now up to you to **believe** and receive what God has already done. Think, **believe,** confess, and receive every promise in God's Word.

Believing Exemplified

Each of you possesses the ability to attain health and wealth!

Believing Exemplified

Have you ever heard of John Brookfield? He is a modern-day example of **The Power of Believing**!

John Brookfield recently pulled a truck weighing 24,000 pounds a distance of one mile in 1 hour and 23 minutes.

Brookfield rolled up one-quarter mile of steel cable nonstop in 59 minutes with no help.

Brookfield and Jon Bruney pulled a semi-truck weighing slightly over 32,000 pounds one mile in 1 hour and 36 minutes.

Brookfield tore 100 decks of plastic-coated poker cards in half in 2 minutes and 15 seconds.

Brookfield performed 1,200 kettle bell snatches in 1 hour using a 53-pound kettle bell.

Brookfield bent 520 60-penny nails in 1 hour and 42 minutes.

Brookfield used a 50 pound sledgehammer for 1 hour and struck a tire 30 times per minute non-stop throughout that hour.

While Brookfield possesses the strength to accomplish these great feats, his true power comes from belief in his strength! Each of you reading this book possesses the ability to attain health and wealth! I challenge you to exercise **The Power of Believing** by standing on the Scriptures and promises given in God's Holy Word and follow the principles outlined in this text.

Summary

Satan knows how to take God's blessings and counterfeit them to deceive and render God's people helpless and hopeless. When Satan tempted Jesus in the wilderness, he even quoted the Scripture to Jesus, always twisting and distorting the Scriptures to accomplish his purpose. Hosea 4:6 warns, "My people are destroyed for lack of knowledge." May the inspired message of this book transform the life of the **believer**.

Remember three very important principles:

Believe in God and love God.
Believe in yourself and love yourself.
Believe in others and love others as yourself.

Follow these necessary steps to **believe** correctly and to receive Godly results.

- Speak out loud your desires.

- Speaking it before you have it is a vital part of **believing**.

- Be careful what you confess. Confess only that which you truly desire.

- Write your vision and desires down on paper. Place that paper everywhere you possibly can as a continual reminder to help you stay focused.

- Stay focused on your goal. Each day see how many people you can touch. Pass the message on to others so they can be blessed.

- Always remember to give God the glory for all things.

Believing is the most important key to walking in God's abundance. God has given you **the keys of the Kingdom of Heaven**. You have the ability to unlock and release the bounties of Heaven into your possession if you will only practice these precepts. You now have the answer to releasing unto you more than you can receive or even imagine.

Stop, do not wait another minute! Start living as God expects you to live. Living the life God intended for you to live is as simple as just

Summary

believing. After all, without faith, it is impossible to please God. This new way of living can govern your health, finances, and relationships, if you will simply **believe** the Word of God. You change your life by **believing**.

Read the Scriptures at the beginning of this book every day of your life. Continue reading these Scriptures until they are imprinted in your mind and heart. Read this entire book once a week, for at least ninety days, until the revelation of these Scriptures transforms your life. Then, see what God will do. God can only do what you **believe** and confess. **Believe** and confess, and your life will be transformed. When this book's message transforms your life, send the author a note and share how it changed you. Contact him at wdholt@foryouinc.com. Share this wonderful, transforming message with others.

"Heaven and earth shall pass away, but my words shall not pass away."
Matthew 24:35

About the Author

Dr. Winferd Holt

I grew up on a farm in Horry County, South Carolina. My father, Huger Thomas Holt, and my mother, Estaleen Causey Holt, did not have a formal education. Their desire was for me to receive a good education. They worked hard on their farm to provide me with that education.

I attended Wake Forest University and earned a Bachelor of Science degree. During my time at Wake Forest, I married my high school sweetheart, Mary Lester Sarvis. While attending Wake Forest, our first child was born, a daughter named Mary Winiferd (Wynne) Holt. After graduating from Wake Forest, I entered the Medical College of Virginia School of Dentistry. While attending dental school, I worked hard and graduated with the highest academic record ever posted at that time at the Medical College of Virginia School of Dentistry. After graduating from dental school, I developed a very successful dental practice in my hometown of Loris, South Carolina, and the Lord blessed us with our second child, a son named Winferd Dale Holt, II.

I accepted Christ as my Lord and Savior while in high school. His hand has been on my life even when I was undeserving of His touch. My faith walk has been greatly influenced by the writings of E. W. Kenyon. After years of walking with God, I have come to understand more fully who I am in Christ and how I am to experience the fullness of what Jesus did on Calvary. In the past few years, God has shown me that nothing is more important than believing the right way, and that right way is to believe the Word of God literally and not be swayed by circumstances or appearances. In other words, believe the Word and expect supernatural results.

After eighteen years of practicing dentistry, God led me in another direction. That journey led my wife and me to found ForYou, Inc., an international company. After much prayer and pure belief, we began an incredible journey of faith. We have seen the hand of God do unbelievable things, things the world said could not be done. We stepped out on faith and simply believed God. We believed even when our church family was saying you should not do that. Our mission is to operate this business based on the principles found in the Word of God. Over the past twenty-five years, God has increased our desire to emphasize the necessity of operating and living

About the Author

in the realm of the Word of God. We have discovered that believing is the key to unlocking the Kingdom principles.

Satan will fight you all the way. You must simply believe God. Satan has tried to take my life three different times. One of those times was in 1974 when a horse reared up and came down with his metal shoe striking me on the top of my head. I never felt or knew anything. My wife was watching, and she said I fell like a dead man. My eyes rolled back in my head; my mouth gaped open. My life was gone. I was not breathing, and I would not respond. They administered CPR, and my first awareness was at the service station where we were filling the vehicle with gas since we were on our way to the hospital. I asked my wife, "Where are we going?" She replied, "Be still and do not move. You had a little accident." I reached up to touch my head, and it was covered with blood. The hospital x-rays showed I had a compound fracture of the skull. I was transported immediately to The Medical University of South Carolina Medical Center for surgery—a two and a half-hour trip. The surgeon removed the shattered bone as soon as I arrived. God's miracle was the lining of my brain was not even scratched; therefore, no damage. I never had any pain, never had any infection (although a dirty towel used to wipe the horses down was the only towel available to cover the wound), and never showed any side effects. I now have a plastic plate the size of a silver dollar piece to cover the fractured area of the skull.

As believers, the Bible tells us in Psalm 34:19, "Many are the afflictions of the righteous: but the Lord delivereth him out of them all." In these latter days, "The thief (Satan) cometh not, but for to steal, and to kill, and to destroy (God's people)," John 10:10. Yet in that same verse, Jesus gave the promise, "I am come that they might have life, and that they might have it more abundantly." As a Sunday school teacher, my students are suffering many afflictions from the enemy. I see the same thing as a lay speaker as I speak in various churches. I believe much of this suffering could be corrected with the proper belief system.

I believe God has given me a vital and relevant message for today. This message can dramatically change the lives of people who will simply believe the Word of God in every area of their life. I pray that this book will cause a person to live the abundant life now.

Notes

Notes

Notes

Notes

Book Order Form

Please send me _____ copies of ***The Power of Believing*** at $10.99 per copy.

Add $5.00 for shipping and handling per address.

South Carolina residents add appropriate sales tax. Sales tax is calculated on the sum of the price of the book plus shipping and handling, $15.99.

Total enclosed $ _____

Name _____
Address _____
City _____
State/Zip Code _____

Please make all payments in U. S. funds. American Express, Discover, Visa, and MasterCard accepted.
Name on Credit Card: _____
Credit Card Number: _____
Expiration Date: _____

Send to: Dr. Winferd Holt, 3980 Main Street, Loris, SC 29569

www.ingramcontent.com/pod-product-compliance
Ingram Content Group UK Ltd.
Pitfield, Milton Keynes, MK11 3LW, UK
UKHW041944230426
12048UKWH00008B/117